THE LANGUAGE
of SAXOPHONES

SELECTED POEMS *of* KAMAU DAÁOOD

POCKET POET SERIES *No. 57*

CITY LIGHTS
SAN FRANCISCO

Cover photograph © Max Schwartz
Cover design by Yolanda Montijo
Book design by Elaine Katzenberger
Typography by Harvest Graphics

Library of Congress Cataloging-in-Publication Data

Daáood, Kamau.
   The language of saxophones : selected poems of Kamau
Daáood.
         p.   cm. — (Pocket poets series ; no. 57)
   ISBN-10: 0-87286-441-3
   ISBN-13: 978-0-87286-441-2
   1. Jazz—Poetry.   2. African Americans—Poetry   I. Title.
II. Series.
   PS3604.A325L36 2005
   811'.6—dc22

                                          2005000900

Visit our web site: www.citylights.com

CITY LIGHTS BOOKS are edited by Lawrence Ferlinghetti and
Nancy J. Peters and published at the City Lights Bookstore,
261 Columbus Avenue, San Francisco, CA 94133

ACKNOWLEDGMENTS

This work was supported in part by:
California Arts Council Fellowship
Durfee Foundation Fellowship
Cave Canem Fellowship

Some of the poems have appeared previously in the following publications:

Catch the Fire (Riverhead Books); *360 A Revolution of Black Poets* (Black Words); *Songs of the Unsung* (Duke University Press); *Ascension* (Ascension Press); *Liberator of the Spirit* (Ascension Press); *High Performance Magazine; Village Voice*

As well as on the following compact disks:

JazzSpeaks (New Alliance Records); *Searching for the One* / B Sharp Jazz Quartet (M.A.M.A. Records); *Jazz Poetry Kafe* (Black Words); *Leimert Park* / Kamau Daáood (M.A.M.A. Records); *Horace* / Dwight Trible (Tongo Productions); *Living Water* / Dwight Trible (Passin' the Vibe Records)

Special thanks to the World Stage and Leimert Park family as well as Beyond Baroque Foundation for their support. Thanks to Elaine Katzenberger, my editor, for her efforts and belief in this book, as well as the great City Lights Staff. Thanks to my friends, community, teachers and ancestors. All praise and thanks to the source of all.

For my wife Baadia, in all her radiance,

For Lady, Precious, RaSudan, Naimah and Akhenaton,
my children,

For Ameera, Omari, Oni, Lil Lady and those to come,
my grandchildren,

For Debbie and Talib, my sister and nephew,

For all my family with love.

Thank you for the love and support in spite of myself.

CONTENTS

THE LANGUAGE
of SAXOPHONES

THE LANGUAGE OF SAXOPHONES

prana moving through time signatures
bop blown through a wormhole
aimed at the earlobe of God
pondered DNA in saxophone solos
rising over the hills of the lips
whirling wonder
articulating the language of bruises and bliss
in urban lit fires of spirits
places and spaces of being
if you been there
you know there

matrimony of head and heart
child conceived beyond reason
entwined with the moment
revelation and swearing
staring at the core of sound
undressing

the blues man
closes his eyes to sing
cotton balls and chains

bibles and juke joints
slurring the edge of english
where speech collides with guinea
vocal chords plaited like
nooses knots and braided whips
rise from the throat
remembrance of cruel tattoos

collected oratories of solitude
sometimes the eyes become the ears
sometimes the hands sing of galaxies
pure music of sign language

a new star
born in the mouth
stinging the ears with glory
holy ghost
spun from a tongue
sweeter than the grapes
on the frontline

sacred act
to vibrate the air
and shape meaning
write on the wind
with reverence

the will of a mind
seasoned in the wanderings of silence
a language
common as the song of water

truth is
some of us live hard
understand the nuances in a moan
know when the saliva is about to boil
know when glass is about to break

understand
the thread of the wind
the treasures buried in smiles
pure laughter of rain
or how thoughts harden
into things seen and touched
to have experienced the malignance of hatred
constructed as house or world
to have been to the center of pain
and given a speech on tolerance

drape these notes
in history
save its shadows for remembrance
etched in the petals of illuminations

fragrant as a pillow of answered yearnings
no longer shackled by traditions or tribe
fearful of change or difference
free of the gangs we have joined
chanting
in the language of saxophones

December 2004

---

*prana, the breath of life, the vital force

SPEAR RITUALS

■ ■ ■ ┃ ┃ *1970-1979*

ANCESTRAL ECHOES

from sapphire's womb they slid
queen mothers and forefathers
these are the shoulders that have carried us here
these are the backbone to our giant tree
they speak like tongueless bells
light marching from the bowels of time
their voices piercing the denseness of history
proverbs melt like warm music in our ears
they are the builders of civilizations
and we are their children
sculptors of pyramids, inventors of science

we are seeds rooted in the cosmos of African clay
spears thrown into the future
crescendos over the dung hills of
stale hyena's madness
we are temples and walking shrines
earth people with earth songs
blacksmith dancers and village drummers
sunburst and naked flowers
we drink palm wine and eat cassava and yam
our lips drip with the mango nectar

we give praise that we may hear these voices
moving like a bamboo flute song in silence
honest work is our worship
we place like a bed of gold
before God and those now gone from sight

in the wind we learn
that die-hards do not die
they only echo throughout the universe
as light

DANCE OF THE NIGGANESE DANCER

a sermon in memory of Ernest Cojoe

I

hey pookie,
here the atmosphere
like glittered clouds, loudspeakers around our heads
raining psychic pins and needles
mental puppet strings, electronic witchcraft
skyscrapers built on the foundation of maggots
schools rooted in lies
we are wrestling with bomb droppers
mind mutilators, planetary hoodlums, thugs with computers
drunk off melanin, paper lynchers, corporate cockroaches
military maniacs, industrial idolaters

they are slinging ink at us
popping us upside the head with magazines
attacking us with electricity
bombarding us with bullshit
barbarians in the sanctuary
fools farting at the most sacred part of the ceremony
these men that rule the world

who sabotaged the global dance
with picnic baskets full of guns
and hearts pumping pus
these beings void of reverence
for stars and trees and people

it was the darkest hour
and the rivers were urine
and the food unclean
and the sky beat them down
with her grayness
in the east the coldest winter
in the west the earth shaking
a parade of plague across the land
the proponents and protectors and defenders of lies

the real, surreal and madness the norm
many tried to lose their shadows
by jumping into the bottom of the bottomless pit
and sought happiness on the weekend
but could not find it
so they sat around and watched Babylon on TV

and then there were those
who were persecuted because they stood erect
because they smiled and spoke firmly

living in an hour when deep breathing is unlawful
but their hearts beat in time with a cosmic clock
and what they were could not be erased
for their seeds were planted snugly
within the rich truth of earth
and the eye of the Most High
would watch over their growth

II

Kojo
they cannot kill this spirit
Kojo
they cannot kill this spirit

it is not the human but what lives in the human
it is not the human but what lives in the human

Kojo
they cannot kill this spirit
Kojo
they cannot kill this spirit

it is not the human but the human's work
it is not the human but the human's work
not the human but legacy

Kojo
they cannot kill this spirit
Kojo
they cannot kill this spirit

the i become the we
the i sacrificed on the altar for all
the work it must be done

III

a swollen black belly full with the new age song
a whole note bellowed from the loins of truth
to mold and shape its face in the image of divinity
a child is born carrying the faces of its ancestors
between its shoulders

know that our sweat in the dew of noon
is the nectar of spirit
is the strong dark wine of experience
and our sperm is directed at the womb of the world
and our hearts are sculpted clay
in the hands of the skilled will

the sun does not stay behind the clouds for long
know this

the i become the we
the i sacrificed on the altar for all
the work it must be done
the i become the we

IV

i come
with word and drum
with sword and seed
with water and rich pot of earth
i come with birds perched on my shoulders
and singing children
i come with flute and strong hands
with vision and health
freshness and light
i come with wind and color
sacred books with blank pages
prepare to write with my blood and sweat
i come with nameless God and universal law
i come to make love and smiles

V

i am the nigganese dancer
the African blood that put the red in the clay of Georgia

exiled in a wasteland
of cannibals and saloons
barflies and wallflowers

i am caught between the roaches and the stars
in my right eye is beauty
in my left eye is pain
i look upon the world cross-eyed
sandwiched between the agony and the ecstasy

the things i see i cannot ignore
i live amongst the suffering flowers
i smell their dying scents
i am a sun boat riding the waves of life
sailing through calm and storm
toward the eternal horizon
stretched out like a platinum snake that swallows its tail

from the ashes
i am the residue
from the burnt remains of the fire of God
swimming in the essence, the pulsating essence
there is wisdom in my nappy hair
there is truth, a perfect stone
i have tasted life with a huge tongue
become the air in my nostrils

cracked the book of life
sat in a lotus meditating upon her pages

i have transformed my shackles into wind chimes
read the Babylon gazette
on the shithouse walls
set aside my books
learning to read
the leaves of trees, the cracks in the street
the bubbles in the water, the wind, the pores of the skin
i distill my past into a potent sap
and set fire to the burden of excess weight
i move swiftly into the new

i have learned from bumping my head
knelt in the sacred garden
embraced the mountain
i am climbing out of a sore
obsessed with health and clarity

i am the madman
the one with the wounded heart
the one who seeks to make things perfect
i proclaim this reality an illusion
i guard the children from the bottomless pit
i am the psychic warrior

a stream a laser beam
i fight the fulfillers of lies
my song grown deep and rich

i am a lone cosmic bullet
headed for the heart of the lie
slaying dragons on the threshold
wrestling stars from their path
boxing witches and devils
vampires and jr. vampires
robots and zombies

they will think i'm a fad
until they find their computers
jammed with toe jam and ginseng root

i am the buffoon
the birds stop to watch me
a lip drummer
for the Lord of creation
dwelling in the solitude of work meditation
i wash my ears in ocean waves
i am the mirror
i give back the reflection
a cosmic tape recorder
my address is written on my heart

i have no anchor
the universe is my home

i am the poor fool gazing at seven butterflies
boogaloo across the sky
i am the shoeblack shit slinger
there is a deep story on my people's faces
their expressions chiseled by the wide gaps
between their laughter

i am the beggar
begging us to be
the journeyman
growing slow like a tree
the scum of the earth
the lowlife
because i sell incense on the street
i am learning to flex the muscles of my heart
here on planet earth serving my time
i am the blind man standing on the corner
singing my song for free
i am the deaf mute piano player
playing not by ear but by heart

i live outside the system on the outskirts
the black bronco buster

trying to tame the desires of the flesh
the soldier training for life's battle
a boy becoming a man
the whole man, the unified man
where i rise above a hard
and transcend a dollar bill
my sight pierces glamour

i am a grain of sand contemplating
the nature of the universe
the farmer
preparing the soil
so my seed can grow rich in Jah's abode

i am burning love tonight, yes
i am burning love tonight, yes

the smoke dance
light of incense flame dance
glow dance
perfume of honest sweat dance
i am the naked dancer
the naked dancer
child of God
mumbling bastard
reaching for the light

i am the lover, lover, and singer, love
spirit man, spirit man, music man
invisible saxophone in my hand, in my hand, in my hand

i am peeling off the slimy veil of fantasy
i am out to lunch
dining on a wisdom sandwich
the sun in my chest bleeds a red sun river of being
i did not come
to shop from the merchants of illusionary things
i am a butterfly seeking
the pollen of the flower of life
and when my spirit hardens
and when my spirit hardens
all will see the reality of the intangible

i swim upstream
beyond the hostile eyes
i swim upstream
beyond the switchblade tongues
i swim upstream
against the faddish waters
and neophyte polluter farting in the sun

oh this is a heavy movie, y'all
i feel like a pallbearer

and the world be a casket
oh won't the divine playwright
lighten up the script

oh pain watch us grow old before your eyes
oh a child has such a perfect voice
the streets are full of rapists
the news sad comedy
but, artificial flowers are dying

why do we hide the quality of hearts
why do we frown so
who make the children ugly
who are we trying to impress
the bacon brains are cause for tears

please take a seashell to your ear and meditate
clean up for spring, clean up for new life
do a heavy dance in the cotton fields
and smell earth songs
the songs so bittersweet the sugarsweet tears
dancing with a raindrop
like colors moving on a hummingbird's wing

sing a song
for those that suffer

sing a song
for those that suffer

sing the uplifting song
for the mess over, the trampled on
part your lips for peace
suck in the wind and blow out a song
for the children who will never ever
sing you black bird sing

sing a song
for those that suffer
sing a song
for those that suffer

for gas head, the gap tooth
for grandma rubbing her aching joints
let the grunt and the moan come out
the screech and the scream come out
the woe and the heart eruption
sing you black bird sing, yeah

oh carnival spirit
oh festive spirit
lift high this tattered voice
i am a hoarse bird singing

a mean blues tune
hear this carribean funk
i am swinging on a banjo string
sliding on a sweat-wet conga
a choir of nappy-headed children
singing a la la song
the purity of this work song
can bust the devil's ukulele

i speak of richness, our richness
our reason for being
the wind slapping our face with love
universal law flowing through us
i speak of unborn light, future's light
if you can see it you can be it
if you can see it you can be it
i speak the pain of struggle
that brings the deepest joy

i speak of jubilation
i speak of jubilation

praise and thanks to the Most High
live in you and i and i
Lord of creation

praise and thanks to the Most High
live in you and i and i
Lord of creation

praise and thanks to the Most High
live in you and i and i
Lord . . .

THE LIP DRUMMER

for Dadisi Sanyika

I

with the raw edge of language
he creates song
here where old cars come to die
and streets soak up blood like sponges
here where agents from the devil's butthole
suck the life
from the souls of our children
and leave them with
ears tuned to orchestrated static on radios
uzi rhythm played on the snare drums of the midnight air

with the raw edge of language
he creates song
word, as a force for uplifting, resurrecting
word, as a force for healing, awakening
word, as the space around silence
building blocks for the song he is trying to sing
this wind he sucks and blows
this heartbeat that he must master
the essence of the work is healing

rebuilding a circle
promoting the life force
unearthing the raw jewel
uniting the scars to make something beautiful

the healer speaks
only after the tongue has been washed
wingless egos with bald heads
surrender to the winds of humility
the skylark of truth
the healer does not shine from silken threads
but from some inner tapestry
his words shine, his silence shines
he is wrapped in a sense of knowing
his life a sacred drama
you will find him where he is needed
there is a presence
the feeling of being whole again
the essence of the work is healing

II

he spoke with a black tongue
and a pure heart
street corner orator on a global soapbox

offering lip drumming and sound-sculptured folktales
about the naked light pressed against our minds
his skypiece tilted toward God
washed with the tears of the mothers
dyed red with the blood of the fathers
a crown sunburst flaming
naps snapping their fingers
to the beat of the pure heart
past
dixieland pickaninnies
dribbling basketballs and watermelons
cakewalking old smokeys, kinky sambos
buckwheat jigaboos, junglebunnies
spineless, bootlicking handkerchief heads
above the rusty blades of midnight cutthroats
a parade of stereotypes
perched on the brilliance of dignity

we listened and inhaled the light
as best we could
yet still our mouths could not speak
to form the true name of God
beating in our chest
brain dead zombied out
bozo clones clowning responding

to the woofers and the tweeters
smacked upside the head
with the color bars and the newsprint
simon says, monkey see monkey do
and the black tongue with the pure heart spoke
a slave of higher purpose
with two feet on the ground
mind puking up impurity
engaged in unlearning
a soul with diarrhea
flushing out the germ of imperfection
honest sweat in the sun

their names we wear like clown suits
laughing at our origins
they know who we are
it is us that have forgotten

and on the cosmic scale
the sacred text of the wind
their history betrays them
their forefathers' works condemn them
they built their house with whips
they spread their God with guns
these scholars masturbating in libraries
glue shut the pages of history with their watery semen

their names we wear like clown suits
laughing at our origins
they know who we are
it is us that have forgotten

a people's mistake
they wear as scars
and only the light renews
noble action in the light
those who seek their faults and fight
those who work on self
change scars to stars, change scars to stars
the earth is the proving ground of the spirit
restore the memory of wholesomeness
the retaking of sacred vows
this the black tongue
with pure heart said . . .

RELIGION OF DREAMS

for Rahsaan Roland Kirk

the blind man walks and talks
in his sleep
and acts from the substance
of dreams
out of the blackness
came the light

stars behind sunglasses
bells and whistles
three horns stuck in his mouth
hurricane in the chest
blind man with a wheel
on the tip of his cane

a note held four hundred years
breathing through the ears
blues scholar, slave chants, field hollers
funky as a gutbucket
church pew climbing out of his horns
horn stuff with ragtime,
horn stuff with boogie

Rahsaan, Rahsaan
close the eyes and
the third eye opens
heal with sound vibrations
historian of feelings

blind warrior on the frontline
blind boxer in the ring
wearing the champion's belt
hitting you with a flurry
bebop upside the head
the truth faced, squarely
the beauty the blind man sees
vibrations, echoes, light

Rahsaan, Rahsaan
the blind man walks and talks
in his sleep
and acts from the substance
of dreams

LIBERATOR OF THE SPIRIT

■ ■ ■ ■ *1980-1989*

WORLD MUSIC

one thousand saxophones
seven hundred kotos
eleven machetes dripping sugarcane
three hundred violins
six hundred fifty bagpipes
fresh cut bamboo screaming
nine thousand birds in prayer
two hundred mechanics
grease buried beneath short fingernails
eight hundred sitars
seven ten-foot gongs

one million tearless children in Ethiopia
three hundred hammers
two hundred saws
ten holy men in subways
twelve divine mothers in wash houses
fifteen hundred shovels in South African mines
forty-nine koras and seventeen balaphones
seven thousand and three assorted drums
seven thousand and two assorted hearts
fifty steel drums

ten thousand midwives carrying fresh fruit
seventy purple banjos
half a million Muslims chanting Quran
six thousand birds of paradise
one hundred golden fishermen's nets
three thousand silkworms
eight thousand waterfalls
seven trillion ten billion six hundred and
one million two hundred and four tubas
and one black chopstick

LIBERATOR OF THE SPIRIT

John Coltrane was a freedom fighter
Liberator of the spirit from the shackles of form . . .
John Coltrane was a freedom fighter
Liberator of the spirit from the shackles of form . . .

expanding beyond the boundaries
blow away decay
stale forms collide with freshness
patterns of life
woven sound into tapestry of meaning
ears chewing mind food

John Coltrane was a freedom fighter
Liberator of the spirit from the shackles of form . . .
John Coltrane was a freedom fighter
Liberator of the spirit from the shackles of form . . .

life coming out of a saxophone
shit and rainbows
shit and rainbows

raining, raining
diamonds the water
diamonds the water

emerald jade the lemon grass
emerald jade the lemon grass
silver the wind
silver the wind

jasmine
jasmine

sapphire the black earth
sapphire the black earth

a flower in the moon's nappy hair
a flower in the moon's nappy hair

our God lives in the people
and the stars swirling

our God lives in the people
and the stars swirling

shit and rainbows
shit and rainbows

gangster rainbows
rebel rainbows

life is a saxophone
life is a saxophone

raging rainbows
coming out the lips of a horn
golden tongue of fire
inspire us higher
ears lick the air
sensitive radars
searching the airways for truth
eyes peering into life seeking justice
hands able and ready
to serve a righteous cause

music music
all is music
music music
life is music

music music
all is music
music music
life is music

the Most High is nameless
faceless and whole
beyond time
filling space completely
our bodies holding breath

learn to harmonize with the changes
strengthen ourselves into polished beings
carry the song more perfectly
beautify movement, speech and thought
watch our hand gather scars
discover the beauty carved in silence
feel our eyes growing deeper
experience the spasms
of uncontrollable laughter
watch our children sleep in peace
struggle to understand our mates
learn the secret of night
embrace the magic of morning
paint the cheeks with tears
study herbs and stars
turn ours ears away from
devil singing with a
turd stuck in his throat

music music
all is music
music music
life is music

music eaters
released into the blood stream of the wind
probing the globe

hear this polyrhythmic logic
priest slinging tone color with principles
scientist whirling song with reverence
pouring beauty into our timelessness

city babies born in a space age
urban babies born in a rat maze
be careful when you sing your song
they are unlawful in this land

c sharp, b natural
music music
all is music

b sharp, c natural
music music
life is music

the sternness of spirit
erected in the light of unchangeable law
the courage to work on self
to make monument of self
silken gut songs
bubbling from the diaphragm
communities of consciousness
world music
soothsayer scatting landscapes
wailing hidden places
circles burst
listening hard for origins lullabies
celestial solos
sailing galactic wailing
smoke-a-rooney
bebop fingerpop from the top
anti mental slavery choir
avant-garde be on guard
to extinguish the self
into the golden cinders of the sun
in an air of smiles
hit this heart with a sledgehammer
it will not be moved
it stands firm in rainbows
heritage nappy and fertile

descendants of die-hards
on the ascension

becoming whole notes
not 16th notes
not 8th notes

becoming whole notes
not quarter notes
not half notes

becoming whole notes, whole notes . . .

the silence roars majestic praise for listeners
pouring truth in open ears

life is a saxophone
playing a sacred song

rapture uphold the eyes
a cosmic view, a love supreme
magic, magic music
shining warriors dance
leaping shooting star
fire leap prancing sun
rescue those lost in mirrors
and stuck in bubble gum

wash the mind with music fresh as piss
from a brand new baby's bladder
translate the nectar of scholars
pondering the universe
into music infants understand

let us see the world that clearly
let us know the world that well

it's a matter of believing
beyond believing
knowing
it's a matter of seeing the future materialize
as we see it
it's a matter of organizing
the raw materials of life
into images as we
will them
not wish them to be

it's a matter of motion
a matter of discpline and sweat
a matter of developing human potentials
in ourselves and others

as we organize our space
we organize our lives

as we organize our space
we organize our lives . . .

the motion is the music
the energy is the music
the constant change is the music
the struggle is the music

blowing glowing grooving moving
expressions impressions
pointing to a higher place
break the silly staleness
the loud farts
the sound pollution
the lies

bust the rat's eardrum
if you can't sing
you better learn to hummmmmmmmmm . . .

John Coltrane was a freedom fighter
Liberator of the spirit from the shackles of form . . .
John Coltrane was a freedom fighter
Liberator of the spirit from the shackles of form . . .

THE LAST PSALMS

for Billy Higgins, master drummer

Papa Jo Jones, Philly Joe Jones, Jo Jones, Joe Jones
Papa Jo Jones, Philly Joe Jones, Jo Jones, Joe Jones
Papa Jo Jones, Philly Joe Jones, Jo Jones, Joe Jones . . .

we set the stage for prayer
the heart of a man as a drum
we make ablution with smiles
an offering of the joy of our sweat

"Praise him upon the loud cymbals.
Praise him upon the high-sounding cymbals.
Let everything that hath breath praise the Lord."

praise him upon the skins of drums
breathing metal and wood, fire in the hands
performing surgery with polyrhythmic heartbeats

praise him upon sundials filling time,
molding silence, thunder and bells
wind chimes and gongs, tin cans

and sticks on oatmeal boxes
children's laughter

praise him upon planets, cymbals swirling
flying saucers more than
mere keepers of time
space creators, rhythm liberators
a winged clock, birds clapping
a blind man tapping in time

praise him with drumrolls, moorish modes
staccato rhythms with batá drums
and sanctified tambourine
fueled by black-eyed peas and greens

praise the Lord with shoe-shine rag pops
bouncing boxspring bed rhythms
foot stompin' and finger poppin'
hambone and hand jive
on the world stage
bass pedal buckdance
and high hat tap dance

praise him with raindrops
good feelings and higher mathematics

black cowboys on a camel magic carpet ride
righteous marching rhythms

because after the whip pops, bomb drops
and the hoodoo bandits and the backroom action
after the blood-soaked money and doo doo breezes

the smiles of the knowers swing
there is no God, but God

Papa Jo Jones, Philly Joe Jones, Jo Jones, Joe Jones
Papa Jo Jones, Philly Joe Jones, Jo Jones, Joe Jones
Papa Jo Jones, Philly Joe Jones, Jo Jones, Joe Jones . . .

DEEP RIVER IN HER VOICE

for Lady Day

divine daughter speaks
in tongues of royal chanters
a purple lotus blossom floats
in a rich red pool of Bessie's blood
at the fork of some southern road
seven faceless eunuchs
in blue, white, red pinstripe suits
gardenias pinned to their lapels
with golden hypodermic needles
sucking money from cash registers
with silver straws

cigarette smoke becomes fine incense
whiskey turns to dew
and she rises on the stage wailing
and from her mouth
an eastern wind swirls and swells
like some wild bird's freedom song
screaming melodic nectar
about the nine zillion times

she carried the world within her womb
for nine months,
round like a whole note in space
and gave birth on this very same stage
she is peeing on
purification ritual of sweat,
with tears we wash her feet

the spirit got her rocking, got her stomping
spirit got her shaking,
knocking the dust from heads and hearts
engraving the story in our consciousness

the wind become song
the trees bent over
listening to the earth's heartbeat
ebony pearls, sculptured African love songs,
mystery in city clothes
hurling rainbows,
transforming saloons into temples
toes, seeds germinating
dancing soil sounds rich with story
earth songs, mountains of memory
nooses hanging from trees
turn to harps and blues guitars

river's lullaby, nourishing laughter and hope
strength in harmonious groans
triple dip in life's pains and pleasures

and from her full lips the sun rises
spilling onto a stage of light
this fire warming the room
healing us with
cool honey and truth massaged on eardrums
by an ancient flower held
in the Most High's hand

BALM OF GILEAD

for Lester Young and Billie Holiday

she graced him with the title of Prez
he crowned her Lady Day
they stand together on the stage
these cousins of sorts and songs
holy water drawn from the same well
a common bond of knowledge
a raw nerve runs deep
so sensitive to the touch
overdose of feeling, life full and aching
gardenia floating on a lake of tears
porkpie hat flattened by the weight of the world
this friendship sailing in a silver chalice of hemlock
pearl necklace of broken hearts
gold watch of shattered dreams

the saxophone turns sideways
smoke and warm fire oozing lava river
gazelle dance in Kansas City air
Lady Day's angelic satin whining secrets in your ear
the torn edge of raw silk surrounded by rainbows

from light filtered through a whiskey shot glass
the cool sound is pain shackled
and made to walk a straight line,
the pure tone of truth

the tongue full of Cupid's arrows
the language an army of bent blue notes
at the foot of the ear
there is little money for the players
only spirit and history
the sweat from hot light, the ocean of applause
shadows in lonely hotel rooms
the laughter and the smiles
of photographs

she graced him with the title of Prez
he crowned her Lady Day
and at the church
Lester laid out in a casket
like a saxophone in its case
Billie pleaded to sing
this offering, this final gesture
but they, the bloodsuckers
the holders of her cabaret card,
spit no on the purest request

shit on her gift and
stepped on her heart
once again
they carried her off to a saloon to sedate her
in four months she would follow Prez
off of the world stage
into the spotlight
seeking the Balm of Gilead
you dig?

BIRD DROPPINGS

for Charlie "Yardbird" Parker

In ancient Egypt, it is said that at the time of judgment
the heart is weighted against the feather of truth.

a trail of chicken bones leads to the bandstand
bird droppings on the world stage
messages from a higher realm descend
here at the center of the universe
microphones, spotlights
men entwined with their instruments like lovers
and in the air
passion and feathers

Bird, half hawk, half nightingale
is perched on an alto saxophone in a garden of song
Mingus Bud blossoms
Miles of Dizzy Monks chanting to the Max
a bouquet to the world
flowers pressed on black vinyl
flying saucers for the ears of the future to decode
bebop bloodlines encircle the heart

now is the time
a man in a wrinkled five-hundred-dollar suit
sweats diamonds and
exhales the ancient futures
up from the gut memory, the foundation
the fire of the raw soul dripping
the source of song
up from the pure bowels of heaven
the deep well, the naked nerve of feeling
the ground truth, the stone, the root bone
the other side of the belly button up

hummingbird fingers flutter on keys
butterflies and sparks cut the darkness
the essence distilled to
feather of truth
floating in the air
a star rises from the Kansas City soil
air loops, twists, precise zigzag, straight ahead
fat rainbows quantum leaping tempos
ballads that will bust a heart
silken lyricism coated with urban paint
hieroglyphics translated into birdsongs

now is the time
the moment turned inside out, bleeding

made to sing its best song
now is the time
music is a mystery in the sound a history
the life divine
now is the time
bird swinging on strings
blowing pyramids in the face of the sun

genius will ride a human being
higher notes the epiphany of children's laughter

genius will ride a human being
low notes discovered
in a crown of thorns,
racism wrapped around heads
like bloodstained turbans

genius will ride a human being
a man, radar ears and an enlarged heart
tears in the New York snow

genius will ride a human being
fire him up, use him, burn him out
then seek a new soul to exploit
for the greater good

a horn laid to rest heart broken
silence, dust in pawn shops
nailed to a cross with
rusty hypodermic needles
our minds kissed
our ears left golden
and in the morning
we hear birds
and we remember
bird droppings

ARMY OF HEALERS

I

art as life
the raw material to sculpt joy
and meaning
religion and science in a mix
graceful movement in space
a martial dance in the midst of disease
sacred time, a weapon
word and light, strong medicine,
action prayerful, move wisdom
breathe consciousness, think sculpture

this is an army of healers,
physician heal thyself
and radiate, radiate

II

knees on a worn prayer rug
soaked with dew
handwoven moments
simple wool and cotton

wrap around a human heart
ancient offerings
rosewater poured over
the mouth of singing bamboo
speaking in sun tongues
pushed against the fragile wind
solitude as music
played on the labor of flowers
parched spirits
voices so old
they crumble in the dance of incense
and climb in the mind
through the nostrils
warriors with stacks of mail
left in the rain

III

the flowers have eyes
if they had mouths
their song would slay us
they know the chains on our tongues are rusty and blue
slow suicide that stretches over a life span
if not free by the courage of motion
thought kindled in the fireplace of experience, unleashed

raw enough to see the flowers looking up at us
with no mouth in which to slay us with song

IV

arthur learned to finger the saxophone
by picking cotton with bloody fingers at the age of five
he moistens his reeds with dreams he collected
as he sang spirituals by his grandmother's knees
when he plays his soul spills out from the bell of his horn
sometimes he vomits flowers sometimes barbwire
it depends on what his heart had to stomach
the night before

arthur was born in america
and raised in the housing projects
he did not speak english
just broken pig latin and fluent saxophone
and a little spanish he learned from his neighbors

this is an army of healers,
physician heal thyself
and radiate, radiate

V

urban tribal scars
decorate the cheeks of the young scholars
endangered as those in tar pits
savage red streets rip the life of innocence
impotent parents bleeding in the shadows
swimming in bills and dogma

here the buildings lean and peel
flattened to the ground
by the fat butt of smog
hieroglyphics sprayed on walls
precision lobotomies executed
through the ears
with organized static
from ghetto blasters
young mind left bleeding
naked
in front of snot-covered TV's
in a garden of suffering
you do better talking to trees
for at least the trees talk back

this is an army of healers,
physician heal thyself
and radiate, radiate

> *The Church is becoming alarmed by the*
> *number of people defecting to God.*
> —*Bob Kaufman*

> *Every person prays in their own language.*
> *There is no languge that God does not understand.*
> —*Duke Ellington*

Buddha played the Lord's Prayer
on Krishna's flute
to the batá drums of Shangó
in praise of Allah

Sufi dervish swirl in Jah's ecstasy
dressed in white
transcending with tambourines
in storefront churches
chanting "Om" in tongues
dreadlock women in saffron robes
quote Muhammad with bibles and beggar bowls
with hands clutching prayer beads

missionary Zen masters
chew peyote at the foot of the Kaaba

singing Amazing Grace
holy rollers study the kabbalah on Persian rugs
practice yoga in the pyramids
as a shaman sits in a lotus in front of a computer
translating bird songs into Swahili

monks make ablutions in sacred waterfalls
and dance ancient dances in praise of Ra
incense and candles
roses and sacred books
rum bottles and Tibetan gongs
at the foot of a blind man
painting icons
on the walls of skyscrapers

Buddha played the Lord's Prayer
on Krishna's flute
to the batá drums of Shangó

ONE GOD
ONE WORSHIP
ONE SACRED PLACE
ONE HOLY BOOK
ONE WORSHIPPER
ONE

WOUNDED WITH A BLESSING

■ ■ ■ ▌ *1990-1999*

SUNBATHING IN MY TEARS

i rise in the morning
with angel samba sunbathing in my tears
i shed my dream garment of spirit paintings
i lift my voice on sails of prayer ships
i reach out and touch the earth
and chisel at the face of day
sculpture of love, dance of the deep place fire shining
i want to know the surrender of the pure singer
the glistening of the platinum gut
i want to melt in babies' laughter and cleansing herbs
polished in the hands of story
poems tattooed on the eardrums of unborn hummingbirds
i offer this as truth of magic
as humble worship, as naked wisdom
breath of incense, burning steel of will

i rise in the morning
with angel samba sunbathing in my tears
i swim these rivers of asphalt
light for the mind of the slave
change bringer, chime maker, invisible circle chanter
in pain the fruit of the heart is squeezed

the nectar sweet, silk sheet of the wind kiss my face
dry the salt of this day's madness
slay me with beauty
resurrect me with duty
mighty is the ocean in my eyes
i rise in the morning
with angel samba sunbathing in my tears
wrap me in rainbows untie me with song

LEIMERT PARK

my heart is a djembe drum
played upon by the dark hands
of a fifth street cappuccino
my invisible turban is an angelic saxophone solo
the sidewalk is hardened mud cloth
massaging the soul of my feet
i do West African dance steps
reflecting the sun off my Stacey Adams shoes
i stand on the o.g. corner
tell old school stories with a bebop tongue
to the hip hop future
i see new rainbows in their eyes
as we stand in puddles of melted chains

visit the black sensei
the grumpy voice
wrapped in juju
warrior spirit guarding
room full of stereotypes and ancestral story
a moor in a porkpie hat
stands with a video camera
in front of a stained glass musician

i lowride on a zebra
in front of Kongo square
we clothe ourselves in sun
and Africa by the yard
handwoven the fabric of the lives
we sculpt

there are trees in Leimert Park
under which old men do divination
with the bones of dominos
Degnan a river, a nu Nile, on whose banks
young poets sharpen their hearts
on the polyrhythms of Billy Higgins' smile
on the world stage where Tapscott fingers
massage your collective memory
at the crossroads
a vision is shaped by a woman
who labored as a maid
and gave her wages to her village
here where children play double-dutch
with dreadlocked ropes
and believers wash the streets
with a mother's tears under kente sky
vomit up your television set
take a deep breath and exhale your fears

scrub the tombstones of those who died young
until they become mirrors
in which to see yourself
take long stares at your hands
until true love returns to your touch
then touch
stand right in a garment of light

i want to pour poems
into the open arms of your drums
i want to get in between your piano keys
and unleash the healing secrets
i want to stuff your dreams
with a bed of cleansing herbs
i want to wipe the bull's-eyes
off the backs
of your children

LOS ANGELES

the angels here
have pigeons' wings
blue collars
washed in sweat
the common salt
in tears
tongues swirl
in a stew of cultures
singing asphalt songs
in the midst of seagulls
bebop atop
the San Andreas
a humble plate
of beings

MANTRA

a head open to the worlds
and spoon-fed light
an oath swelling
on the lips

a clock that
looks like a mirror
reflecting a
fat sound seated
in a highchair
turned inside out

the tenderness
in true overstanding
the tireless ritual of stones
and blank books

dream shapers chiseling
butterflies
out of crayons
imprisoned within the
dew locked
within a spider's web

a wind full of naked secrets
resting in cocoons
on the drums
of our ears

a lesson of dust
from the breast
of dinosaurs
a monk
and a marxist
in meditation
using a
Coltrane riff as
a mantra

HEALER'S LAMENT

I

lament for the poet
swallowed by the cracks in the street
flowers for the dead musician
strangled by a bill collector
in a bank parking lot
prayers for the painter
drowned in white acrylic
what words have we for the dancer
split apart in indecision

sacred clock, holy field of light
martyrs, healers
why does beauty wade through dung
calloused and unnoticed
why is the sweat of the heart invisible
why must love ache and peel in loneliness
like orphans in the trash bins of the world
dogshit on the jugular vein
the masterpiece submerged in the abyss of blood
a painting hung on the wall backwards
lost to the eyes of babies

why do sons die before their fathers
why do daughters give birth to children
with faces that add up to zero
as we sit in concert halls with chastity belts and ear muffs
promoters of robotic music
cancerous and vile
mouth stuffed with tombstones
mutilators of dreams

II

battering rams spitting graffiti
on uterus walls
watermelon seeds swelling in asphalt
traffic jams and drive-by shootings
of pistol-whipped lovers
panting in the shadows
dancing in the spotlights of helicopters

woe to the lost fruit and all its nectar
woe to the suspended souls spinning
in an unformed universe
crumb snatchers slip into a world of ice
wrapped in nightmare of AIDS tattoos
and crack smoke sunglasses

no eyes smooth, no navel smooth, no mouth smooth
only nostrils plugged with the funk
of dreamless men
tripping over the length of their lives
scripted with a pitchfork
at the edge of flame

the place where they came together
is the place where they fell apart
they look at each other
in the void of cracked eggs
chanting the pledge of allegiance
to a pitbull with a billy club
on an ocean of crack vials and uzi shells
planned parenthood discussed
in a think tank
Hitler became an American citizen
and hope floats in an empty pack of Kools
sailing down a gutter river
of five million 40 oz. bottles of malt liquor
filtered through the bladder of a ghost
that is about to lose his pants

III

holiness uttered from the bastard's lips
suck fire from ocean of stars in a drop of blood
to have been to the place of torment
and return with a badge of scars
and praise on the lips

in the silence you will understand
the ears turned inward
the work sits
on the desk of the heart
under the light of mind
the soul sweats
extract wisdom from a tear
when the horses of desire are tamed
ridden to new horizons
then you will move
through the body of God
as a healing agent
instead of a
disease

WING

gypsy
told me
half my fortune
wrote it on my liver
with a dream
decoded
the mystery of evening
in candle wax
deciphered
the religion of poets
into an unfinished
bass solo
talked to whales
from a mountaintop
and left
me
pulling poems
from my past
like a dentist
standing
in the light
with just
one
wing

FOR PAUL ROBESON

there is something in the voice
solid as the head of John Henry's hammer
polished to a noonday brilliance
there are roots in this voice
wrapped around the blue core of earth
utterances decorated
with finger paintings
by outstretched hands
of the world's hungry children

speak for us
we that come
calloused and scared
bodies shaped and marked by toil
holding down the edges of the world
with our labor
we pull and twist and pound and cut
we push and rub and split
and fashion the raw material of this earth

fight for us
the sunkissed, the sea dweller,

those wrapped in night
those sweating in holes
that do the work that others refuse

we fold the clothes
stack the books and bricks
chart the stars,
shaping wood and words
working with paper and pipes,
losing fingers for others' profit

arms full of flowers and
sweet herbs
shoe covered in mud,
hand covered in blood,
we wash the dead
and make the bread
we know the sacredness of dishwater
the weak, the hungry, the homeless,
the tired, the sick, the lonely
those of us that work
but can't pull jack shit,
let alone a jack rabbit
out of a hat

meat ass on the hook of industry
smoked booty in the fire of exploitation

sing to us in a million tongues
about the blood and wind and sun that bind us
about our common struggle
in this voice is courage
pure undefiled
testosterone
in the state of service
at the spot of clarity
in defiance of false masters
in the face of tyranny
toe to toe with a lie

this voice a backbone
that grows like a garden
bursting from the chest
beyond sound and time
there is something in this voice
and it is oh, so,
precious

DJALI

for Bob Kaufman

I

in the shadows of blue volcanos
the broken fingers of ancestors strum
koras emitting frankincense

II

i sleep with a Senegalese blanket
of turquoise sound over me
it stops the helicopter blades from slicing up my peace
spirits sitting upon an orchard of notes
sprinkling my dreams
with promise
as i wait in this celestial cocoon for silver wings
remembering the lesson
dealt
in the sacred mud

III

each morning i read the newspaper
and weep into a pot of coffee
i muffle my whispered screaming
with the music of the masters
i find religion there
rocking in ecstasy
to the heartbeats of loved ones
i open my door and
begin swinging like young Muhammad Ali
i rest between rounds
on a bus stop bench facing east
i fight to knock out a nightmare
in broad daylight
the bus driver is a Sufi saint
who only lets you ride
if you got incorrect change

the Zen bell has rung

DJALI II

for Bob Kaufman

his heart is a blue bulletproof vest
new orleans sufi with a jewish moniker
clutching the fury of silence with pregnant tongue
bouncing up and down like a child that has got to pee
a stone in the mouth of a ten-year fast
the alphabet cut up with scissors
in a coffeehouse of painted shadows
merchant marine counting stars
backwards from infinity
writing poems with an ink pen on neptune's back
glowing on the sidewalk in a circle of stares
holding a new language in his mouth with
his wisdom teeth
only pronouncing new words when he is alone
and he's always alone
but we know he exists by the poem-stained streets
and the neat pile of human dung
on the business section of the newspaper
in the alley near an invisible liquor store
where they say if you are still enough

you can hear him give poetry readings
about the same time
some folks go
to church

BLAKEY'S STICKS

I

I want to give Art Blakey's drumsticks
to some child without a father
to use as chopsticks
to pick the stars from beards of giraffes
sitting on milk crates
in front of liquor stores

men who have swallowed grief
and extracted the secret of seasons
men who have suffered and
found the stillness of a Mali morning
riding the red eyeball of
a hurricane
on a street corner in Watts

old ones who could stain young minds
with the lips of ancient songs
and make them friends of wisdom

these children of asphalt
blinded by grey and neon

tongue-tied with empty money clips
looking for faint footprints
of their home training

deaf to the voices of the old ones

II

I remember the flags of surrender
waving on clotheslines stretching
across America's abdomen
color dancing in a breeze of ghetto perfume
twisted ballet of Congolese sculpture
song in the Atlantic's darkest indigo
whispering pyramid of bones
at the bottom of the sea

come, ride the backs of purple dolphins
past the ghosts of the present
a spider waiting for you
in a world wide web
wants you to pick cotton in cyberspace
wants you to wear a bow tie
of yellow police tape
wants you to snort

the chalk lines on asphalt
thru a didgeridoo

children of asphalt
refuse to wear
the psychic beehive hat
swarm of conceptual killer bees
awaiting you at dawn
here where I is the first
and only letter in the alphabet

children of tarmac
seek out the old ones
with gold at the tips of their tongue
you will know them
by their scars

III

they will call you
when your mind is drifting
in the current of trends
your mouth spilling words
belching like an empty slot machine

their words will hit you
like a crowbar of light

they will pull back the concrete
show the naked breast of the earth
and you will cry
for the children on the milk cartons
and you will cry
for the butchered babies of Rwanda
and you will learn to ball your fist
and swing in the right direction

seldom are a young man's eyes
an old man's eyes
seldom are they skilled
as souls aged in struggle
you know this life
from looking at her face
light and the body of light
gloried in the fragrance of doers
builders, those that carry others
until they can carry themselves
the fire of truth
is an eternal flame

I want to give Art Blakey's drumsticks
to some child without a father

a moment of silence please

a choir is screaming eulogies
to a stadium of deaf people
is a grave plot
a hole in the earth
or a plan?

THE MEN

for my sons, RaSudan and Akhenaton

I

deep the space between father and son
deep the place where chests meet
fragile the air carrying words
from the male heart
difficult the eyes in meeting

father, pass the story
and tell the secrets
son, humble the ears and cling
to the wings of the words
that carry the torch
of your son's song
on the tongue of your father
your grandfather speaks
of his father
to your unborn grandchild

clip the wings of the ego
that hinders flight

tip toe with clenched fist
in this hour of the breaking of chains
deep is the conversation
of bearded hearts
sacred the word that dwells there

II

in the firm gripping of hands
the silence of the male air
folklore of barber shops
shielded speech
muscle and stance
the music our fathers whistled
sweat and hue
hats that cover the head
minds full of stars and wonder
the spit shine of noon
the deep thighs of night
hard voice of reason
in the long scar of memory
you will find it. . . .

III

i will show you the beauty of my scars
they are concealed beneath my skin
some given me by your mother
to teach me to see myself
i have many scars
i pull them out when i am alone
i read them like scripture
i bathe them in prayer and memory
i offer them to you as light

JEWELED ZERO

i sit atop an earthquake fault
meditating on the faults within
jukeboxes full of sanctified flamingos
dancing like James Brown on one leg

wake up the insomniacs
of tambourine buttocks
halos soaked in lavender castanets' sweat
lamentation of laminated sorcerer
hoochie coochie torpedos
limping fetishes
sequined
and bare-knuckled rhumba

modal phantoms
sipping muzzled uranium dreams
droning syncopated prophesy
about the jeweled zero
dipped in lacerated turquoise
flirtations of belly buttons
gyration of hollow whispers
midnight sacrificial wounds

and in the morning the buzz of silence
the thick air of poverty
sliced up by the geometric dance of flies

morning in a lonely room
colored in shadows
pierced by dust
floating like tiny dead angels
in rays of light

PAPA, THE LEAN GRIOT

for Horace Tapscott, pianist, arranger, composer, mentor,
community arts activist, beloved patriarch

i am Horace Tapscott
my fingers are dancing grassroots
i do not fit into form, i create form
my ears are radar charting the whispers of my ancestors
i seek the divinity in outcasts, the richness of rebels
i will pray for you on this snaggle-toothed piano
songs for the unsung
whose lineage was fed to sharks in the Atlantic
i will concertize you into trance, here in this garage
conjure spirits that will sing you into remembrance
on this piano so far out of tune it opens doors
to other worlds
i will climb inside this piano searching for our history
i will assemble a choir of unborn voices
to teach you what the future sounds like
i will love you with the warmth of the African sun

i walk these sacred streets
remembering kola nuts and cowrie shells

and how well our uncles wore their trousers
i am Horace Tapscott
and i am not for sale

the eyes look inward as the story is told
voices painted in the dignity of old photographs
we have seen blood on the piano keys
cobalt-blue chains, slurred notes
as truth wells up in the corners of eyes

our richness like honey stuck to the tips of singing fingers
with palms held up in gestures of prayer
smoke thick as frankincense dance on pilgrimage
fade like golden echoes at the porch of our ears
to have seen life moving
smooth as a red dress
on a purple spirit
on a slow yellow day
cracked open the moment
like children laughing
their mouths held wide
trying to catch the sun

remembering when
our ways were straight and rooted

when we did what we had to do
with what we had to do it with

under the sheltering wings of family
walking lines to ourselves with spirit guides
elders correcting children
the way folks held their heads
the gathering of smiles

oh singing fingers, oh swelling fire in the chest
we should know such joy

a thousand eyes watching
children grow next to flowers
as old ones pray over food
where men with shiny shoes
swap tales and work songs
men knotted at the gut level
in a common pool of sweat
remove their hats to pray, remember

and women form bands of healing
quilting rhythms and
tucking them into an ark of stars
sailing through a storm of hardships
deep changes bring out the beauty of a song

where babies hide their fingers
in gray beards
weaving teardrops and laughter
into a bright cloth of collected wisdom
etched in multi-colored ink on memories' wall
love would hover in a room
like the scent of good cooking
and fall down like warm hands
on the backs of travelers
a family was a circle of love
a community was a family
we did what we had to do
with what we had to do it with

oh singing road of destiny,
blanket of night whispers
rose essence and spirit hum
talking wood and flame-dancer
street theater and heart sport
music oozing from each breath
kissing our ears like angels
the sacredness of strife

take time and give it to others
take time and give it to others

the eyes look inward as the story is told
voice painted in the dignity of old photographs
we have seen blood on the piano keys
cobalt-blue chains, slurred notes

i am Horace Tapscott
my fingers are dancing grassroots
i do not fit in form, i create form
my ears are radar
charting the whispers of my ancestors
i seek the divinity in outcasts, the richness of rebels
i walk these sacred streets remembering
kola nuts and cowrie shells
and how well our uncles wore their trousers
i am Horace Tapscott
and i am not for sale

SEARCH FOR THE
PUREST WATER ON EARTH

■ ■ ■ ■ ■ *2000-2004*

ANGEL OF SCISSORS

for Mexican jazz pianist, Olivia Revueltas

I

in the country of hearts
compassion is the common language
in this place
we speak with feeling

a shared space
subtle as the air altered by a wing
or the faint edge of a song softly ringing
gone from the ear
but echoing as an image in the mind
each heart is the center of this world

II

light cutting away the tumor of darkness
beyond these thoughts whispered by jinn
false angels chanting
tongueless sweet poison
invading the birthright of joy

there is light and there is darkness
and then again there is light
lightness
melody of feathers

the sickness of greed
this disease a force in the world
those with their self-importance
not knowing that from the sun
you cannot see human eyes
and our breath has a limited visa

what good are the eyes
that fail one in a garden
what good are the ears
that only hear songs of static
what good is the tongue
that has not learned praise
in the hour when the judges will be judged
on the sweetness of the eyesight of the heart
and worth measured by
the extent of their helping hands

who carries strength?
to darkest rooms
jigsaw torsos of Middle Eastern children

scattered limbs of the Cambodian killing fields
a mother's laughter lost
in the blood-soaked hillside of Chiapas
balloon bellies of Haiti
a cancer victim moaning
in a cardboard box
in an American alley
a billion outstretched hands
"an angel to escort each raindrop to earth"
an angel to catch each tear

BLUE PACHUCA

for my mother, Delores Keyes

There I go, there I go, there I go, there . . . I go. . . .
—King Pleasure

Blue Pachuca,
hair of Manila in blue light
you have taken your mystery with you
gone like the silent flight
of birds of paradise

lady of sorrow
you are why sad music makes me happy
why i run to the arms of blue tone when i'm in pain
you scatting James Moody in your children's ears
waiting tables in Westwood for twenty-five years
lines from a million smiles creased your face
"How can I help you?"

i remember your morning meditations
of coffee and cigarettes
there at our kitchen table

as i made bell sounds with my cereal bowl
all i knew was that i was safe and warm and loved
i did not know the secrets buried within you

it was always you, standing next to the heater
towers of silver coins from the night before
the cars moving through the songs of birds
as i rub my eyes of dreams

daddy was gone in morning when i rose
he would return in the evening
with his silence, his privacy, his introversion
his love was large, always quiet
i feared his voice
it had such power
the beauty of his hands surrounded us
never abusive
even when holding his belt like a whip
wisdom unfolding in stinging lessons

i remember laughter in our house
Jesse Belvin or Dinah Washington would tell stories
from our speakers
and my little sisters and their little white dolls
auntie said when you were young you were Pachuca
you hung out with the Mexicans

because in Santa Monica in the '40s
there were few blacks around

i wish i knew your bebop and salsa laughter
when you were a free bird singing
and dancing with zoot suits

i never talked to you with the eyes and voice of a man
you left so young

so now i shift through memories
listening for your whispers
for your soft voice of blue light
in the great house of silence

Blue Pachuca
lady of sorrow
your father is from the Philippines
Manila and Africa in your bloodstream
and sailed to me, Negrito

my uncle is my grandfather
your mother is like your sister
raped at fifteen
by her big sister's husband

my uncle cut and gave me fresh sugarcane
my grandfather was a pervert
this man that was two people
who thought he could clear his karma
giving me his old car
and now i suck the sweet juice of the cane
spit out the bitter memory
of his abuse in our family

Blue Pachuca
hair of Manila in blue light
bebop and salsa laughter
you have taken your mystery with you
gone like the silent flight
of birds of paradise
from a vase
of warm tears

DAMAGE

there is a child's hand
in the street
it is small
it should be attached
to a three- or four-year-old
you cannot tell if it is the hand
of a Palestinian child
or Israeli child

you cannot tell if it was blown here
from a suicide bomb blast
or shelling from an Israeli tank
it's just a small bloody hand in the grey of the street

someone weeps
insane with the weight of this image
someone who has held that hand
taught the child to count the fingers on that hand
in Hebrew or Arabic

there is a baby's hand
in the middle of this Middle Eastern road

and you can't tell if the child's parents
read Quran or Torah

it's just there
small and bloody
without a smile and laughter attached to it

so look away

we are told
it's just
unfortunate
collateral damage

THE LIVING WATERS

the living waters upon the lips
at the center of the concept is life
if the earth had breasts they could be here
if the world had a womb it would be here

in this place of beginnings
the idea of race as a misnomer
the world is One
divided into many
the breath and the landscape of possibilities
the cleansing thought of circles
our seamless existence, cause and effect
the blindness of bad thinking
dressed in a suit of dogma
thought that makes things ugly
an evil twist of nature,
a false belief
drive the hands to act
upon the earth improper
a stray note in a song

in a perfect moment we could be one
the richness in this moment,
more than drums and stale rituals
more than flag waving and staking claims
a family regrouping for joy of the planet
a school of perfecting the soul,
we memorize the words to the human song
heart beating as common music
the breath and the land that connect us
excuses are the links to our chains

we could dance
on a dirt floor
of color and splendor
each fingerprint makes its contribution
if the earth had breasts they should be here
the world's children nourished
from wisdom of oneness
hear the rhythms of light
shed your chains and dance
drink of the living waters
wash your face in the tears of humanity
with mind, hand and heart
will a new world
into being

SWEATING PAISLEY

for Jimi Hendrix

harness lightning
leaping dolphins off a rainbow bridge
guitar plugged into a cosmic amp
melting blue flames in his hands
mud on the voice
delta poetry dripping from his guitar
maps drawn with sticks in the electric mud
sound moving
skyward

at first the music was invisible to my ears
i had never heard an electric prayer before
never knew that guitars
could open doors
like saxophones

lifted mind from a prison of labels
false walls that separate us
defining things

that need no definition
just is

screaming strings
harmonize in high frequency
bathe our ears in a field
of sound
bending light
new connections

I searched Seattle
for the pillow
that held Jimi's head
dream catching,
plucking love from the nest
of broken hearts
the borrowed weeping
of blues men
singing into empty bottles
of perfume
with their processed hair
of crows

prayer and electricity
in an awesome room
mud and the spirit shaped into a man

black gypsy
sweating paisley
under stars
dancing rainbows
in the night

THE PIANO IS A DRUM FOR TEN FINGERS

for Omar Sosa

pepper sauce
poured over European melodies
hard swing in Latin flight
waves of sacred guts unleashed
slave chants soaked in flaming sugarcane
slice the wind whistling pass my ear
the songs of ancient machetes

i remember the rum dancing in the old man's voice
and the fish scale played on upright pianos
the curved new rhumba
on the strong calves of dark women
sea and sand and sun spun songs of children
weaving through the blue chants of birds

salsa blood rushing through buffed fingers
that holds the sweat
rolling like midnight marbles
off the backs of lovers
dry in the morning
red at the edge of the world

like ancient trumpets,
Moorish echoes
rising smoke from a Cubano cigar
ringing, flamingo light of silence, ringing
wood and bones
ringing metal string
exalt the secrets tucked in eyes
that learned painfully
that transform memory to wisdom

fire of spirit, light of spirit,
lift us over oppression's door
lift the golden bones of our ancestor
from deep book of the sea
in tattered fisherman's net
lift us on language of drums,
barefoot and barebutt, babymaking salsa
when the moon is a shakere
infinite pinholes of light
laughing through a sky of indigo
salsa on the mountaintops
dripping, ringing

black beans,
definitely,
black beans

THE WATCH

in the hospital
you horizontal, me vertical

i not wanting to know the time
you handed me your watch and ring
you had never done that before

i sensed mother's breeze in the room

they said you had congestive heart failure
they told me it was like breathing underwater
you said you were tired

mother silently chanting in my ear
"tell your father you love him, tell your father you love him"
my vocal cords hardened asphalt
a mute saxophone

in this silence
this perfect space between us
i would like to think you heard me
gone from the body
that carried the song

WAR

I

at the ragged edge
of midnight
sits an albino crow
with dog tags
flapping its bloody wings

a billion mothers
knees bent in a lake of sorrow
from every corner of the world
pray for morning's light

we are told
that war is the circumcision
needed to enter the gates of peace
by leaders with blood on their hands
but no dirt under their fingernails

those that call the shots
are not the have nots

those that call the shots
are not the ones shot at

those that end up dead
are not the ones that led

II

i hear people screaming
on the other side of the world
bloody choir of wailers
burnt vocal cords
reaching for the heavens
spirit thrown from bodies
splattered on walls of history

i hear people screaming
on the other side of the planet
screams rising through the ether
moving upward
proliferation of smoked yearnings
it is men's minds
that pain the flowers
drive the hands to evil
coordinate the screaming

screaming choir of orphans
orchestra of blue widows
screaming ensemble of maimed moaners
and mumbling fathers
chanters of seared flesh
and burning futures

i hear people screaming
on the other side of the street

there are those in fine suits
that cause the screaming
in their chest a ball of maggots
they live all over the planet
speak with many tongues
profess different faiths
drunken from a notion
of predominance
they are cannibals
the sweat of the poor
fills their swimming pool

the screaming is their music
screams that harden
into gold

III

and our earth says
i have seen this
before

WEEPING AT THE MAILBOX

Poetry is not art, it's an illness.
—Cleveland Simms

my work is invisible
i weave words
to loud silence
violins, shaman's woe
build homes with phantom nails
made for tomorrow's eyes
internal sweat
i close my eyes
and go to work
calloused
beneath eyelids
no one can see me
perched on splendor
singing in the center of a thought
or counting babies' toes
from afar

poetic license is fake i.d.
they refuse to cash my dreams

at the bank
this is why i am
weeping at the mailbox
the world keeps sending me letters
telling me money
is God

others do not see the work i do
they only see me staring at a spot in space
they do not know how difficult it is
to move these words around in my head

maybe if i leave the house at seven
and return at six
i could fool them

i hear voices
i see ghosts
i see the possible future
i feel the invisible thread
that connects us

maybe if i checked into
a hospital
perhaps
they could

make me normal
help me find a real job

because
this is not
my last
poem

ZILLION TAMBOURINES

a zillion tambourines
splashing against
the green wall of silence
we nurse our wounds
in the pure waters of dolphins
cleanse our back
of the sores of the city

creditors with hi-tech daggers
tell us who dressed these plantations
in skirts of steel and asphalt
where we must pry pearls from life with a crowbar
trying to balance light between shoulders
in the midst of dung stacked in rectangles
where the head can become
a cesspool of wrecked slave ships

we have come to sit in the blue chair
fish in pure stream of consciousness
watch the hummingbirds
folding the day with their wings

watch pastel sunsets whisper
as leaping swordfish bull's-eye the open sky

fifty drummers in a circle of flowers
weaving in and out of brown rhythm
helping to remake us
a mind in trance
nodding in revelations of fireflies
fire in the pillow bosom
of Fannie Lou Hamer
we rest our head in a cloud
trying to retain
the iron spear
of Robeson's
baritone

Kamau Daáood, performance poet and community arts activist is a native of Los Angeles. He is the author of two chapbooks, *Ascension* and *Liberator of the Spirit*, and a widely acclaimed spoken word CD, *Leimert Park*, for which he received a PEN Oakland Award. He is also the subject of an award winning documentary film, *Life is a Saxophone*. A former member of the Watts Writer's Workshop, Daáood honed his skill as a "word musician" for the Pan African People's Arkestra under the direction of pianist and composer Horace Tapscott. In 1989, he and master drummer Billy Higgins co-founded The World Stage in the Leimert Park area of Los Angeles, and under their leadership this storefront performance gallery became Los Angeles' black creative epicenter. In addition to numerous awards for his civic and artistic activities, Kamau Daáood has received a Cave Canem Workshop/Retreat Fellowship, a Durfee Artist Fellowship, as well as a California Arts Council Fellowship. He is the director of the performance group An Army of Healers, and more information about him can be viewed online at www.KamauDaaood.com

Printed in the USA
CPSIA information can be obtained
at www.ICGtesting.com
JSHW082213140824
68134JS00014B/598